FROM GOD'S ARMS
TO MY ARMS
TO YOURS

MICHAEL McLEAN

SHADOW
MOUNTAIN

Photo of Michael McLean by Butch Adams. Interior photos from Photos.com, Brand X Pictures, and Shutterstock.

Cover and interior design by Shauna Gibby.

Visit us at ShadowMountain.com

Library of Congress Cataloging-in-Publication Data

McLean, Michael, 1952–

  [Songs. Texts. Selections]

 From God's arms to my arms to yours / Michael Mclean.

     p.   cm.

 ISBN 978-1-59038-493-0 (hardback : alk. paper)

 1. Contemporary Christian music—Texts. I. Title.

ML54.6.M38F76 2007

782.42'17100268—dc22   2007026516

Printed in the United States of America

Worzalla Publishing Co., Stevens Point, WI

10   9   8   7   6   5   4   3   2   1

INTRODUCTION

*Y*ears ago I had an experience that changed my life forever. I wasn't looking for a change, didn't anticipate it, and certainly had no inkling of where it would lead me. I was invited into the world of adoption by a young unwed mother who asked me if I could write a song that she could sing for the couple she had decided to give her baby to. Her choice was a childless couple, married nearly a decade, and from her point of view, they were perfect. She had a feeling this was the best thing she could do for her soon-to-be-born child, but she needed a song to seal the peace of her decision.

Her fear was that her baby might grow up feeling that if his own birth mother would "give him away," he must not be worth much. She was also deeply concerned that the child would resent her decision if he didn't know how hard it was for her to make, and how much it was motivated by love.

The song that came from that request was titled "From God's Arms to My Arms to Yours." A few days after the baby was born and placed with the couple who would raise the child as their own, I sat at a piano in a recording studio and accompanied the birth mother as she sang her heart out. She had a little snapshot of her baby clipped to the music stand next to the lyrics of the song. Never have I felt more emotion packed into a recording session. I didn't know then that I had been firmly placed on a path that demanded the creation of this book.

After the release of "From God's Arms to My Arms to Yours" in 1990, I began to hear from families around the world that were either on their journey toward adoption, reminiscing about adoption, seeking closure, or pleading with me to express their perspective on this most personal and tender of subjects. The letters, phone calls, conversations, and e-mails led to the writing of what I called my "adoption suite"—three "sweet" songs from three separate points of view: "From God's Arms" (from the perspective of the birth mother); "The Gift We Could Not Give Each Other" (about the journey of couples unable to have children of their own); and "Yours" (from the point of view of an adopted child).

For more than a decade and a half I've heard the most remarkable stories from those who have been a part of the adoption process, and I've realized that there would be *more* songs helping me to understand the many sides to adoption. "Hope Hiding There," "Hardest for Me," and "Something Perfect" all resulted from that additional exploration, and with each of these songs I found myself celebrating those who were making the journey.

The songs in this book have been born from years of listening to those who've been on this path before you, with the hope that the music might stir some honest and real place inside that wants to be a part of the expression of this miracle.

My first thought when I created this book was that it would be given as a gift to those participating in adoption. But I've come to know that as you search your own experience and write it down, it is a gift to yourself as much as to those with whom you may choose to share it. It may find you singing your own versions to the songs. (The included CD has all the songs recorded with vocalists, plus instrumental versions of those songs that you could sing to, or record a narration of your choosing.) Who knows, you may make a DVD with this music as the underscore to your first birthday wish or a soliloquy of gratitude and love at a meaningful anniversary.

We've also set up an online community, FromGodsArms.com, where you can download sheet music, share your own experiences, and meet others who are involved in the adoption process. Please join us!

I've always believed that songwriters don't own these songs we write, we simply hear them first, and try to find ways to pass them on. This book is just one additional way for the song of your life to find a way into the hearts of those you love most. It reminds them how much they matter, and that, in truth, they are never alone.

THE CHOICE

*W*hen you think about it, adoption is as much a miracle as birth itself. Maybe more so, when you consider that for everyone involved it starts from a place of impossible choices: nearly unbearable fear, haunting doubts, interspersed with glimpses of hope brought into partial focus only when seen through the lens of unselfishness. And at the moment of heartbreaking courage, when a selfless choice is made, there are absolutely no guarantees . . . well, maybe one: that every conceivable outcome of the journey had been imagined in sleepless nights and endless days. Still, in spite of all who would say it's beyond possibility that hope or peace or joy could be found, it is.

HOPE HIDING THERE

WHATEVER YOU DO DON'T LOOK DOWN

That's all the advice they can give

But you keep looking down

'Cause you think that's where everything is

IT'S HARDER TO SEE THINGS CAN CHANGE

That night can be conquered at dawn

'Cause the darkness you feel

Is unbearably real and strong

It's just how it goes

No matter what you do

The way through the fog

Has been hidden from view

But around every corner

Though you're unaware

Protected by grace in the face of despair

There is hope hiding there

YOU MIGHT THINK IT STRANGE

HOPE WOULD HIDE

It seems like a cowardly deed

But it's saving its power

for your desperate hour of need

And all of that strength

And good it can do

Awaits being found safe and sound just for you

'Cause around every corner

Though you're unaware

Protected by grace in the face of despair

There is hope hiding there

And ears cannot hear it and eyes cannot see

But hearts are drawn near it if they choose to be

Around every corner

Though you're unaware

Protected by grace in the face of despair

There is hope hiding there

THE PLEA

How do you choose the right parents for your baby? It takes a lot of prayer, a lot of careful soul-searching, and a lot of listening. Some birth mothers talk about "feeling" their unborn infant directing them as they meet with prospective parents. It's not as strange as it sounds. That baby is still half connected to his or her heavenly home. Maybe, if you're very still, you'll hear in your heart something like:

"I know how hard you're trying to make the right choices so my life on earth will be wonderful. But I really want you to know that your efforts to give me everything a new arrival on the planet wants by way of a loving, caring family bond me to you more deeply than ever. I hope you're getting all this, soul to soul, because I won't be able to say it when I'm born, but I love you. I love you . . . and I understand."

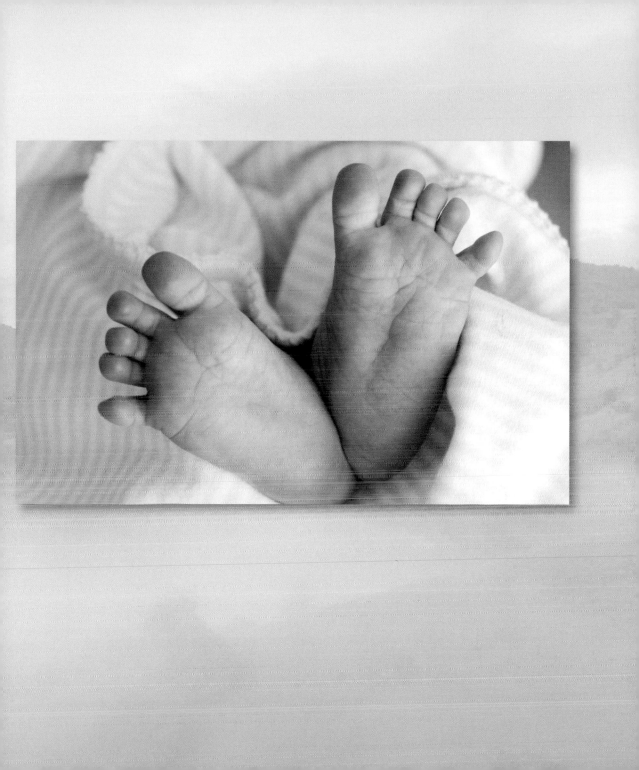

FROM GOD'S ARMS
TO MY ARMS TO YOURS

With so many wrong decisions in my past I'm not quite sure

If I can ever hope to trust my judgment anymore

BUT LATELY I'VE BEEN THINKING 'CAUSE IT'S ALL I'VE HAD TO DO

And in my heart I feel that I should give this child to you

And maybe you can tell your baby

  When you love him so, that he was loved before

By someone who delivered your son

  From God's arms to my arms to yours

Now if you choose to tell him, or if he wants to know

How the one who gave him life could bear to let him go

Just tell him there were sleepless nights I prayed and paced the floors

AND KNEW THE ONLY PEACE I'D FIND IS IF THIS CHILD WAS YOURS

And maybe you can tell your baby

When you love him so, that he was loved before

By someone who delivered your son

From God's arms to my arms to yours

NOW I KNOW YOU DON'T HAVE TO DO THIS

But could you kiss him once for me

The first time that he ties his shoes

Or falls and skins his knee

And could you hold him twice as long

When he makes his mistakes

And tell him that he's not alone

Sometimes that's all it takes

I KNOW HOW MUCH HE'LL ACHE

WELL THIS MAY NOT BE THE ANSWER

    For another girl like me

And I'm not on a soapbox saying

    How we all should be

I'm just trusting in my feelings

    AND I'M TRUSTING GOD ABOVE

And I'm trusting you can give this baby

    Both his mothers' love

And maybe you can tell your baby

When you love him so, that he was loved before

By someone who delivered your precious one

From God's arms to my arms to yours

THE OTHERS

When a birth mother makes the hard decision that her child is meant to be in another home, it affects more people more deeply than she could ever imagine. Not only is a birth father having to face letting go of this child, but everyone else in their extended families is too: aunts, uncles, cousins, and grandparents. And though the families may support and even be proud of the choice, it's still hard, especially for the grandparents. It means letting go of all the memories they expected to make together—trips to the cabin, cookie-baking sessions, sleepovers, spoiling and applauding and loving. Grandparents have a special place in their hearts dedicated to giving their grandchildren everything they want. It takes true courage and the truest kind of love to be willing to give them everything they *need*.

HARDEST FOR ME

I'd start this out saying
THAT MY HEART IS BREAKING
But that wouldn't truly convey
The depth of my feeling
It's no use concealing
The things I don't know how to say
You'll be leaving and I'll be grieving
A dream that never will be

> *It's a hard test when what's best for you*
> *Is hardest for me*

When this decision
Made such a revision
In plans I held tightly before
My fear was that it wasn't clear to me giving you up
Was really giving you more
'CAUSE ANYONE LOVING YOU MORE THAN I ALREADY DO
WAS HARD TO BELIEVE

> *It's a hard test when what's best for you*
> *Is hardest for me*

It's a taste of the bitter that lets us know better

Why One suffered in Gethsemane

It's a hard test when what's best for you

Is hardest for me

THE GIFT

*S*ome of the healing in the adoption process comes from knowing that one family's unselfish choice will open the door for another family's sweetest blessing. How does a couple take the news that they can't bring babies into the world? How long does it take them to surrender their dreams in favor of God's will? The faith they develop in that journey will help them find the faith they need to raise a child to be all that he or she was meant to be, and the gratitude that comes when such a gift is given is almost beyond expression.

THE GIFT WE COULD NOT GIVE EACH OTHER

When I was a little girl I held my dolls like children

DREAMING OF THE DAY WHEN I'D HAVE BABIES OF MY OWN

When the news was shared with me

That all those dreams could never be

It became the deepest grief my heart had ever known

There's a man who tried his best to comfort me with roses

Promising he'd find a way to make those dreams come true

HE DID EVERYTHING HE COULD

To heal my heart but nothing would

And when it seemed that we'd done everything that faith could do

A wondrous gift was given with a phone call straight from heaven

"There's a child that's nearly due that a young girl's giving you"

She gave more than just one life

When she made of this man and wife

A father and a mother when she gave the gift

We could not give each other.

More than we can ever say

Our hearts give thanks to heaven

Every time we hold this child we feel we hold the world

Words will never be enough to share the way our family feels

But with every breath we breathe we want to tell that girl

NOT A DAY IS EVER THROUGH

TILL WE THANK THE LORD FOR YOU

And sweetness lingers here

In our hearts and thoughts and prayers

You gave more than just one life

When you made of this man and wife a father and mother

And you gave the gift we could not give each other

You have changed our lives forever

ONLY YOU AND GOD ABOVE COULD GIVE THE GIFT OF LOVE

We could not give each other.

THE MOMENT

*Y*ears of waiting. Months of planning. And now, in one matchless moment, the miracle at last occurs. There is so much love in this place, and it's pure and it's true because none of the people in the room at this moment are as concerned about themselves as they are for one precious baby. Do all children who come to this earthly home get to feel this?

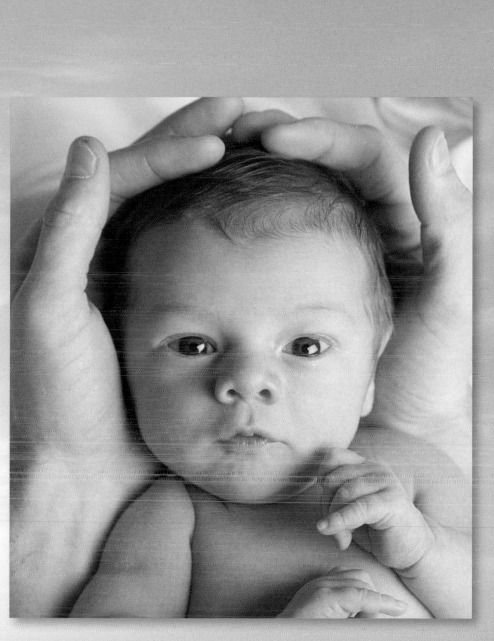

SOMETHING PERFECT

There's an ache that's missing today

There's an emptiness that's been filled

THERE'S A CLOUD THAT'S LIFTING AND DRIFTING AWAY

There's a ragin' storm that's been stilled

There's a joy that's real

There's a wound that's finally healed

There's a future replacing a past

There's breath of new life in the cast

And there's something perfect

Happening here

And this moment will bury

The mountains of fear

And through countless tomorrows

It won't disappear

This something that's perfect

Happening here

No one knows, so no one can say

That tomorrow all will be well

Will the brightest promise that shines on today

Shine tomorrow? No one can tell

But one thing is sure

And will be forever more

WHEN SUCH UNSELFISH LOVE HAS BEEN GIVEN

The world just made more room for heaven

And there's something perfect

Happening here

And this moment will bury

The mountains of fear

And through countless tomorrows

It won't disappear

This something that's perfect

Happening here

HAPPILY EVER AFTER

However it started, whatever pain has been part of the process, the shining truth is that you are a family now. May the hope that you've found at this step of your journey carry you forward into a life of happiness and love beyond your deepest dreams. And may heaven smile on all your choices the way it smiles today.

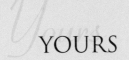

YOURS

You didn't give me your eyes

Or the color of your hair

I'VE CLIMBED THE FAMILY TREE AND FOUND

There's no one like me there

Sometimes I've felt like an alien

That came from foreign shores

But look inside my heart you'll see

I'M YOURS.

You didn't give me these feet

BUT YOU PLACED THEM ON THE RIGHT PATH

You didn't give me my voice

But you taught it how to laugh

You didn't give me these hands

BUT YOU TAUGHT THEM TO OPEN DOORS

Look at all I am you'll see

I'm yours

Do you think the ones who gave me life

Will ever know

The gift they gave to me by letting go

I hope somehow that heaven will reveal

The depth of gratitude I'll always feel

You didn't give me these arms

BUT YOU GAVE THEM A FAMILY TO HOLD

You didn't give me my body

But you've truly shaped its soul

Your love has given me wings

AND HOW MY SPIRIT SOARS

Knowing that I always will be yours

FOREVER AND FOR ALWAYS

I am yours.